D0096075

READY! SET! RESEARCH!

YOUR **FAST** AND **FUN** GUIDE TO WRITING RESEARCH PAPERS THAT **ROCK!**

MARVIN TERBAN

SCHOLASTIC GUIDES

READY! SET! RESEARCH!

MARVIN TERBAN

SCHOLASTIC REFERENCE

AN IMPRINT OF

SCHOLASTIC

Terban, Marvin.

Ready! Set! Research! : Your fast and fun guide to writing research papers that rock! /
by Marvin Terban.

p. cm.

Includes index.

ISBN 10: 0-439-79987-2   ISBN 13: 978-0-439-79987-4

1. Report writing—Study and teaching. 2. Report writing—Computer network
resources. 3. Research—Study and teaching. 4. Research—Computer network resources.
5. Internet in education. I. Title.

LB1047.3.T466 2007

808.042'071—dc22

2006044279

10 9 8 7 6 5 4 3 2   07 08 09 10 11

Interior design: Kay Petronio
Cover design: Tatiana Sperhacke
Cover and interior illustrations by Richard Smith

Art/photo credits:
p. 36: Jennifer Terban; p. 63: Scholastic Inc./Jim McMahon;
p. 115: David Terban; p. 124: Karen Terban

Printed in the U.S.A.

First printing, January 2007

DEDICATION

· ·

To my dear friend
Kimberly Colen, a
beautiful young woman,
charming, intelligent,
brave, loving, and
deeply missed

CONTENTS

Introduction 8

Chapter 1: **SCHEDULE IT!**
HOW NOT TO PANIC AT THE END 11

Chapter 2: **FOCUS IT!**
THE INCREDIBLE SHRINKING TOPIC 15

Chapter 3: **LOOK FOR IT! WITH THE LIBRARIAN**
FIVE MAGIC WORDS 21

Chapter 4: **LOOK FOR IT! IN THE LIBRARY**
IT'S ALL THERE—FOR FREE! 24

Chapter 5: **OUTLINE IT!**
IT'S AS EASY AS I. II. III. 32

Chapter 6: **NOTE IT!**
GET IT ALL DOWN 39

Chapter 7: **RESEARCH IT! ON YOUR COMPUTER**
RESEARCH SURFING 44

Chapter 8: **RESEARCH IT! WITH INTERVIEWS** "I'D LIKE TO
ASK YOU A FEW QUESTIONS, PLEASE." 51

Chapter 9: **RESEARCH IT! AT DIFFERENT PLACES**
HAVE PEN, WILL TRAVEL 58

Chapter 10: **PICTURE IT!**
WHAT'S A PICTURE WORTH? 61

Chapter 11: **SEPARATE IT!**
FACT VERSUS OPINION 66

Chapter 12: **EXPRESS IT! IN YOUR OWN WORDS**
DON'T BE A WORDNAPPER 70

Chapter 13: **CITE IT!**
GIVING CREDIT WHERE CREDIT IS DUE 72

Chapter 14: **WRITE IT!**
FOLLOW YOUR OUTLINE 81

Chapter 15: REVISE IT!

SAVING THE BEST FOR LAST..................86

EXTRAS

   1. Time Budget Chart 91

   2. Research Calendar 92

   3. Doorknob Sign 94

   4. Sample Note Card 95

   5. Search Engines, Online Dictionaries,
      Online Encyclopedias................................96

   6. Sample Interview Sheet............................98

   7. Sample Survey Form 99

   8. Sample Questionnaire Form 100

   9. Fact versus Opinion Game.........................101

      a. Sample "Fact" and "Opinion" Cards 102

      b. "Fact versus Opinion" Game Score Sheet 104

 10. A Sample Research Report About Australia 105

 11. List of Sources 105

 12. Note Cards on Australia 106

 13. Part of an Outline 109

 14. Part of the Finished Report with Source Notes 110

 15. Part of the Finished Report with Endnotes 111

 16. Part of the Finished Report with Footnotes 113

 17. Part of the Bibliography (and map) 115

 18. A Glossary of Research Terms 116

Index 120

About the Author.......................................124

Other Titles by the Author 126

Notes 127

YOUR TEACHER HAS ASSIGNED YOU TO RESEARCH A TOPIC AND WRITE A REPORT ABOUT IT. NOW WHAT?

SCHEDULE IT!

- You make up a schedule to budget your working time (see chapter 1).

FOCUS IT!

- You decide on a focused topic that interests you (see chapter 2).

LOOK FOR IT!

- You seek out the help of a friendly librarian (see chapter 3).

- You search your school or public library to learn about all the research tools you can use there (see chapter 4).

OUTLINE IT!

- You make up an outline to follow as you do your research (see chapter 5).

NOTE IT!

- You find out lots of neat stuff about your topic and take notes (see chapter 6).

RESEARCH IT!

- You search the Internet for more information (see chapter 7).

- You interview people and visit places (see chapters 8 and 9).

PICTURE IT!

- You gather pictures, maps, and other graphics (see chapter 10).

SEPARATE IT!

- You make sure to separate real facts from people's opinions (see chapter 11).

EXPRESS IT!

- You avoid plagiarism by expressing ideas in your own words (see chapter 12).

CITE IT!

- You show where you got all your information (see chapter 13).

WRITE IT!

- You organize the facts and write your first draft (see chapter 14).

REVISE IT!

- You edit and revise your paper to produce a beautiful finished copy (see chapter 15).

DONE!

Let's get started. Turn the page.

CHAPTER 1

SCHEDULE IT!

OR

How Not to Panic at the End

The ancient Chinese philosopher Confucius said, "A journey of a thousand miles begins with a single step." Your first step is to schedule your time wisely.

Follow the three rules below, and you won't panic as the deadline draws near:

1 Begin now ➤ **2** Work steadily ➤ **3** Finish on time

TIME BUDGET CHART

Suppose your teacher tells you that you have to hand in your paper in about a month. But you have other things to do that month besides researching and writing the report. Let's say you have about 22 or 23 days when you can actually work on the paper. Here's a sample of how you could budget your time. These are only suggestions, of course. How much you can devote to each step will depend on how many working days you have, what else you have to do, etc. There's a blank Time Budget Chart for you to fill in on page 91.

Choose Your Topic	2 days
Write Your First Outline	1 day
Find Your Sources	2 days
Take Your Notes	3 days
Organize Your Facts; Finish Your Outline	2 days
Write Your First Draft	5 days
Proofread; Revise	2 days
Write Your Final Draft; Proofread and Correct It	4 days
Put It Together; Check It Over	2 days
Hand It In	7 seconds

Make your own **RESEARCH CALENDAR** (see sample on the next two pages and a blank calendar for you to fill in on page 92).

- Mark the START! and DONE! days.
- Mark holidays, birthdays, vacations, special events, etc. (days when you'll have other things to do).
- Count the number of working days you have.

SAMPLE RESEARCH REPORT CALENDAR

APRIL

SUN	MON	TUES	WED	THURS	FRI	SAT
6	**7** START! GET TOPIC	**8** FOCUS TOPIC (SEE CH. 2)	**9** FIND SOURCES; TAKE NOTES; START OUTLINE (SEE CH. 5)	**10** FIND SOURCES; TAKE NOTES; ADD TO OUTLINE (SEE CH. 6)	**11** FIND SOURCES; TAKE NOTES; ADD TO OUTLINE (SEE CH. 6-14)	**12** FIND SOURCES; TAKE NOTES; ADD TO OUTLINE
13 PICKLE BAKING CONTEST 9 A.M. TO 5 P.M.	**14** FIND SOURCES; TAKE NOTES; ADD TO OUTLINE SHOW TEACHER WHAT YOU'VE DONE SO FAR	**15** FIND SOURCES; TAKE NOTES; ADD TO OUTLINE	**16** ORGANIZE FACTS; FINISH OUTLINE (SEE CH. 5)	**17** ORGANIZE FACTS; FINISH OUTLINE	**18** WRITE FIRST DRAFT (SEE CH. 14)	**19** WEEKEND TRIP TO DRIPPY CAVES
20 WEEKEND TRIP TO DRIPPY CAVES	**21** WRITE FIRST DRAFT	**22** CANARY'S 3RD BIRTHDAY PARTY	**23** WRITE FIRST DRAFT	**24** WRITE FIRST DRAFT	**25** FINISH FIRST DRAFT	**26** PROOF-READ & REVISE (SEE CH. 15)
27 FAMILY STUFF	**28** PROOF-READ & REVISE (SEE CH. 15) SHOW TEACHER WHAT YOU'VE DONE SO FAR	**29** WRITE FINAL DRAFT (SEE CH. 15)	**30** ANNUAL TURTLE RACE AFTER SCHOOL			

MAY

SUN	MON	TUES	WED	THURS	FRI	SAT
				1 WRITE FINAL DRAFT	**2** WRITE FINAL DRAFT	**3** GRANDMA'S BASKETBALL GAME
4 HELP DAD PAINT THE BIRD CAGES	**5** WRITE FINAL DRAFT	**6** CHAMPION-SHIP BANJO RECITAL	**7** CHECK IT OVER (SEE CH. 15)	**8** CHECK IT OVER	**9** HAND IT IN. DONE! WHEW! RELAX	**10** SLEEP LATE

Don't delay

◎

Start right away

◎

Work a little each day

◎

At the end, shout "Hooray!"

▢ Write in pencil so you can adjust dates.

▢ Cross off each step when you finish it.

Your next task is to **ZOOOm** in on the topic you want to write about. Chapter 2 tells you how. Read on.

FOCUS IT!

. . . . **OR** . . . .

The Incredible

Shrinking

Topic

OK, your teacher tells you that you have to write a research paper. Now the fun begins.

Your teacher can give the assignment in different ways:

Write about . . .

". . . *anything* you like."

". . . a *general* topic that I will assign."

". . . a *specific* topic that I will assign."

"*Anything* you like" lets you think about and choose a topic that really interests you. But it gives you about a gazillion possibilities, and unless you work fast, you'll be petting your dog's grandpuppies before you decide on a subject. A *general* topic that's assigned might be too big, and you won't know where in the world to begin. In order to include everything you find in your research, you'd have to write a

HUMONGOUS

paper.

A good detective (detective = researcher—in other words, you!) uses a magnifying glass to focus on small objects.

So, your first job is to

Narrow down the big idea.

Zero in on something specific.

FOCUS!

FOCUS!

FOCUS!

With the help of your teacher, a librarian, your parents, and friends, plus a bit of research at the library and some sensible thinking, you can brainstorm your ideas and **Zooom** in on a very focused subject. That way you'll have a topic that you'll be able to research and write about in your lifetime.

THE HISTORY OF THE WHOLE UNIVERSE FROM ITS BEGINNING TO NOW

is way, way, way too **BIG** a topic to research — at least 15 billion years too big.

How about just *United States* history? You could start at about 1492, when Christopher Columbus set out for the East and took a wrong turn sailing out of Spain. That's about 500 years versus 15 billion years.

Hmmm. Maybe the topic is still too big. You'd have to include so much about

EXPLORATIONS   FAMOUS PEOPLE   IMMIGRATION
POLITICS
FARMING   GOVERNMENT   INVENTIONS   CITIES
DATES   PLACES   TRANSPORTATION   TOWNS

All that would take a million pages. How about zeroing in on just "wars"? Unfortunately, there are plenty of those to choose from.

You still have to **focus** more. Choose the *one* war that interests you the most.

How about the Civil War? That lasted from 1861 to 1865. That's just four years, not 15 billion or 500. But it's still a big topic. Many huge books have been written on that subject.

FOCUS.

FOCUS.

FOCUS.

Do you like action? How about choosing a famous battle of the Civil War?

ANTIETAM
FREDERICKSBURG
GETTYSBURG
SHILOH
CHICKAMAUGA
ATLANTA
VICKSBURG
SHARPSBURG
COLD HARBOR
FIRST BULL RUN
KENNESAW MOUNTAIN
FORT WAGNER

Wow, that's a lot of battles! How about just the **Battle of Gettysburg**? That's the one that Abraham Lincoln wrote his "Gettysburg Address" about. It's one of the most famous battles of the Civil War—just three days—July 1 to 3, 1863. You can tackle that.

Now we're getting somewhere very specific.

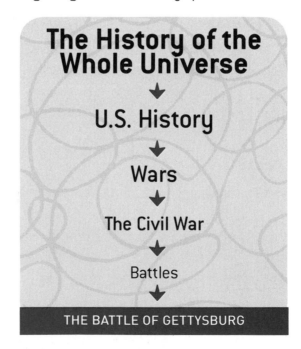

The History of the Whole Universe
↓
U.S. History
↓
Wars
↓
The Civil War
↓
Battles
↓
THE BATTLE OF GETTYSBURG

Here is how you can sharpen the focus of other broad subjects to produce good research topics:

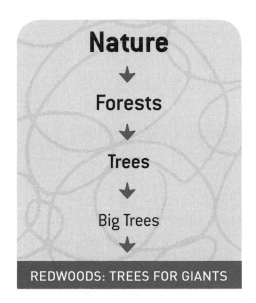

Nature
↓
Forests
↓
Trees
↓
Big Trees
↓
REDWOODS: TREES FOR GIANTS

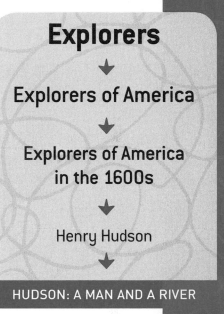

Explorers
↓
Explorers of America
↓
Explorers of America in the 1600s
↓
Henry Hudson
↓
HUDSON: A MAN AND A RIVER

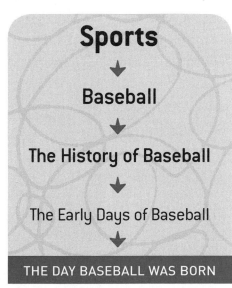

Sports
↓
Baseball
↓
The History of Baseball
↓
The Early Days of Baseball
↓
THE DAY BASEBALL WAS BORN

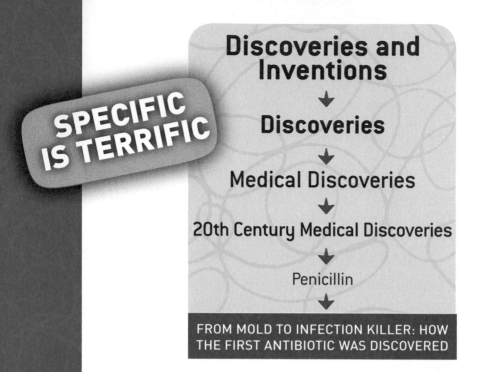

Discoveries and Inventions
↓
Discoveries
↓
Medical Discoveries
↓
20th Century Medical Discoveries
↓
Penicillin
↓

FROM MOLD TO INFECTION KILLER: HOW THE FIRST ANTIBIOTIC WAS DISCOVERED

After you've narrowed down your topic to one you'd like to write about, check it with your teacher to make sure he or she is OK with it. Now you're ready to start your research. Where do you go next? Right to the next chapter. There you'll meet your new best friend, the librarian.

If you have too **BIG** a topic, you'll need some hocus-pocus. Be very microscopic, And **Focus!** Focus! Focus!

CHAPTER 3

LOOK FOR IT! WITH THE LIBRARIAN

OR

Five Magic Words

OK, you've

☑ **set up your calendar** and budgeted your time so you won't panic as time starts running out, and

☑ **narrowed down your subject** so you can finish the paper before you get your first gray hairs.

What next? Easy. Make a beeline for the nearest **library**.

Some school libraries are called **"media centers"** because they have media stuff like CDs, videos, DVDs, and computers. Some school librarians are called **"media specialists"** because they know how to work all that stuff. But if you use the terms **"library"** and **"librarian,"** that's OK.

At the library, you'll find out

- if you're really interested in the topic you chose
- if there's enough information on it to write a good paper
- if you can understand what you're reading

Go up to the librarian, wait until he or she can speak to you, then smile and say:

"Hello, my name is _____."

"I'm in the _____ grade."

"I have to write a research report about _____."

"Can you help me, please?"

Those five words are irresistible to a librarian. Librarians wake up each morning hoping that somebody like you will come in and say, "Can you help me, please?" That's why they became librarians.

To see a list of all the resources that your new best friend, the librarian, will show you, look at the next page.

- The Card Catalog or Electronic Database
- Encyclopedias
- Dictionaries
- Atlases
- Quotation Books
- Biography Books
- Almanacs
- Thesauruses
- Newspapers and Magazines
- Microfilm/Microfiche
- Computer Stations
- Videos, DVDs, CDs, and CD-ROMs

And they're all yours to use — for free! To find out what's in all those books and media materials, turn to chapter 4.

The librarian might also want to know
- **when the paper is due**
- **how long it has to be (in pages or words)**
- **how many sources it has to have**

If you don't know, ask your teacher.

LOOK FOR IT! IN THE LIBRARY

······· OR ·······

It's All There—For Free!

Being a researcher is like being a detective. You have to know what you're looking for and where to find it. You're looking for information related to your research topic, and you're in the right place. Just follow the leads.

Your new best friend, the librarian, will show you how to find books and other materials on your subject that you'll be able to understand. You might be allowed to take some of these things home. Most reference books, however, have to stay in the library.

The library may have a

CARD CATALOG

that lists books alphabetically by author, title, and subject

or it might use an

ELECTRONIC DATABASE

where you type what you're looking for into a computer (*author, title*, or *subject*). Using call numbers, the computer tells you what the library has and where to find it.

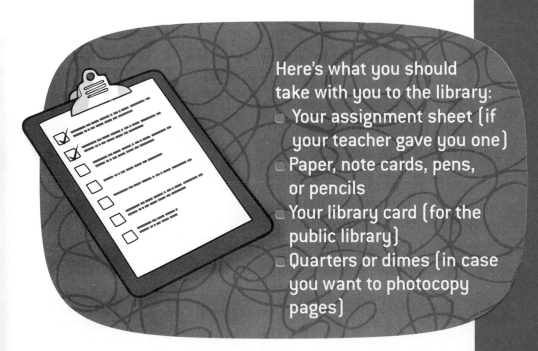

Here's what you should take with you to the library:
- Your assignment sheet (if your teacher gave you one)
- Paper, note cards, pens, or pencils
- Your library card (for the public library)
- Quarters or dimes (in case you want to photocopy pages)

You should be able to locate **at least three or four books** on your topic that you think you'd be interested in reading.

Libraries use the **Dewey Decimal System** to group books into ten main categories. A great librarian, Melvil Dewey (1851-1931), thought it up. He put *call numbers* on books and classified them like this:

> 000 General Works
> 100 Philosophy & psychology
> 200 Religion
> 300 Social sciences
> 400 Language
> 500 Natural sciences & mathematics
> 600 Technology (Applied sciences)
> 700 The arts
> 800 Literature & rhetoric
> 900 Geography & history

If you were looking for a book on rocks, for instance, it would be in the 500 section. Most of the books in these categories are nonfiction (based on real facts and events). The librarian will show you how to use a book's call number to find it on the shelves.

Let's look at what else the library has for you:

◉ **DICTIONARIES** can give you quick definitions, fast facts, illustrations, and tricky spellings.

Look at all the information this brief dictionary entry about Aristotle contains:

Aristotle (384-322 B.C.) Greek philosopher and scientist, one of the greatest thinkers in history. He lived in Athens and wrote about physics, politics, the natural sciences, etc. He was a pupil of Plato and the tutor of Alexander the Great.

• ENCYCLOPEDIAS contain articles loaded with facts on many subjects. From an encyclopedia article, you can write your first outline (see chapter 5). That will help you identify the most important information you have to do research on. Sometimes encyclopedia articles have **bibliographies** that can point you toward other books on your subject. **Key words** in the articles will clue you in to what you have to look up.

In addition to general-interest dictionaries and encyclopedias, there are also many special-interest volumes that you might find helpful. Ask your librarian about dictionaries or encyclopedias of science, film, art, history, computing, slang, animals, space, presidents, Native Americans, African Americans, women, etc.

If you read an encyclopedia article on bees, you'll see **key words** like *pollen*, *nectar*, *comb*, *hive*, *drone*, and *queen bee*. If you research information on those specific subjects, you will gather essential material for your paper.

Never use an encyclopedia as your only source of information, but it's a good place to get a quick overview of your topic.

• ATLASES have detailed maps and charts that give you fascinating facts about places all over the world:

- Locations
- Populations
- Climates
- Products
- Languages
- Religions
- Money
- Geography

There are also **historical atlases** that have maps and facts about places and events from other times.

FROM AN ATLAS YOU CAN FIND OUT

- *what the population of China is* (about 1.3 billion people)
- *how cold it gets in Siberia* (as low as 68 degrees below zero!)
- *what languages are spoken in South Africa* (Afrikaans, English, Ndebele, Pedi, Sotho, Swazi, and others)
- *what four US states come together in one spot* (Utah, Colorado, Arizona, and New Mexico)

● QUOTATION BOOKS contain quotes on many different subjects from well-known people. A quotation about your research topic could add extra flavor and authority to your report.

For a report on art:

"Art is born of the observation and investigation of nature."
— Cicero, Roman author, orator, and statesman (106–43 B.C.)

For a report on computers:

"The great thing about a computer notebook is that no matter how much you stuff into it, it doesn't get bigger or heavier."
— Bill Gates, American computer software manufacturer (1955–)

For a report on pets:

"I like pigs. Dogs look up to us. Cats look down on us. Pigs treat us as equals."
— Sir Winston Churchill, British prime minister (1874–1965)

● **BIOGRAPHICAL DICTIONARIES** contain brief articles about notable people from the past and present. Use these books to get quick facts on the people you want to mention in your paper.

Suppose you're writing a paper about great women athletes. A biographical dictionary could help you make a list of the women you want to research. Here's one example:

ZAHARIAS, Mildred Didrikson (nickname "Babe")
Athlete (especially in golf)
Born: June 26, 1911 (Port Arthur, TX)
Died: September 27, 1956 (Galveston, TX)
United States of America

. . . .

Babe Zaharias is regarded by many as one of the greatest multi-sport athletes of all time. In 1932, she won gold medals for the 80-meter hurdle and the javelin throw at the Olympic Games in Los Angeles. She was also an excellent baseball and basketball player, and she excelled in swimming, diving, tennis, billiards, lacrosse, track and field, and rifle shooting. From 1935 through the mid-1950s, she won many major women's golf championships. Even though she was stricken with cancer in 1953, she continued to play sports almost until her death.

Your library may have specialized biographical dictionaries on artists, authors, inventors, explorers, Native Americans, African American women, and others. Just ask.

● **ALMANACS** are reference books that are published once a year. They contain a huge wealth of fascinating facts, dates, and other useful statistics that go back hundreds of thousands of years.

FROM AN ALMANAC YOU CAN FIND OUT

- The **three biggest oceans** are
  The Pacific (64,186,300 sq. mi./155,557,000 sq. km.)
  The Atlantic (33,420,000 sq. mi./76,762,000 sq. km.)
  The Indian (28,350,500 sq. mi./68,556,000 sq. km.)

- The president of the United States who served the **shortest term** was William Henry Harrison—only one month— March 4 to April 4, 1841. (He caught a cold that turned into pneumonia after giving the longest inaugural address in history without his overcoat, on a cold and windy day.)

● **NEWSPAPERS and MAGAZINES** can contain up-to-date information about your subject that's not in books yet. Old **periodicals** (newspapers and magazines) might be stored on film (microfilm and microfiche) or computer disks (CD-ROMs). Your librarian will help you with these media formats.

● **COMPUTER STATIONS** at your public or school library can help you research tons of material from millions of Web sites on the Internet for free. You may not be able to get some of these Web sites on your home computer (see chapter 7), or you might have to pay for them outside of the library. Some libraries use filtering programs to block certain Web sites. If you try to get onto a Web site and a message comes up saying that it's blocked, ask the librarian for help.

● **VIDEOS, DVDS, and CD-ROMS** that relate to your subject can be fun to watch and will help you picture the people, places, sounds, and events that you need to write about.

And here's all you need to use all this great stuff: your library card.

Now that you've discovered all the terrific research tools at the library, you're ready to start your research. Where do you go now? Right to the next chapter. There you'll learn how to begin outlining your paper.

CHAPTER 5

OUTLINE IT!

OR

It's as Easy as
I.
II.
III.

What is an outline?

- a list of facts and ideas
- in order of importance
- expressed in short phrases

Your finished outline will be your **master plan** for your paper. Without an outline, a research paper would be like your body without its skeleton or your house without its framework. It couldn't stand up.

HERE'S WHAT TO DO:

- **Make an outline** of the first encyclopedia article you read about your subject (see sample on page 36 in this chapter).

- **Add details** to your outline as you do your research (see chapter 6).

- **Use your outline** as a guide to write your paper (see chapter 14).

HOW TO MAKE AN OUTLINE:

Use

ROMAN NUMERALS for the **main topics**
I. II. III. IV. V. VI., etc.
(Put the main topics at the left margin.)

CAPITAL LETTERS for the **subtopics**
A. B. C., etc.
(Indent the subtopics.)

ARABIC (regular) **NUMBERS** for the **details**
1. 2. 3., etc.
(Indent the details more.)

LOWERCASE LETTERS for the **sub-details**
a. b. c., etc.
(Indent the sub-details more.)

Put dots after the numbers and letters.

Capitalize the first word in each entry.

Format of an Outline

I. **First Main Topic**
    A. First subtopic
        1. First detail
           a. First sub-detail
           b. Second sub-detail
        2. Second detail
           a. First sub-detail
           b. Second sub-detail
    B. Second subtopic
        1. First detail
        2. Second detail

II. **Second Main Topic**
    A. First subtopic
        1. First detail
        2. Second detail
    B. Second subtopic
        1. First detail
        2. Second detail

A simple outline will have just main topics and subtopics. A longer paper will have details, too.

Most computer word-processing programs have outlining guides built in. Check yours.

How Many Main Topics?

For an average research paper, **three to six main topics** are usually enough.

- The subtopics must all support the main topics.

- The details must all support the subtopics.

- The sub-details must all support the details.

A Sample Outline

Suppose you have to write a research paper on Leonardo da Vinci. (What a guy!) The first thing you should do is read an encyclopedia article about him.

You might not find enough information to have a lot of subtopics, details, and sub-details. But if you do, try to have at least two subtopics under a main topic, two details under a subtopic, and two sub-details under a detail.

LEONARDO DA VINCI

Leonardo da Vinci had many jobs in his life. As a painter, he created the *Mona Lisa* and *The Last Supper.* He was also a sculptor, an architect, a military engineer, and an inventor of weapons and vehicles, among other creations. As if that weren't enough, Leonardo was also a musician and a scientist.

He was born in 1452, in a little mountain village in the Tuscany region of Italy called Vinci. In 1469, an artist in Florence named Andrea del Verrocchio took Leonardo on as an apprentice in his workshop when he was just seventeen years old.

Starting in 1482, the Duke of Milan employed Leonardo to supervise court entertainments, build military equipment, install a central heating system in his palace, and paint *The Last Supper*.

Over the years, Leonardo filled many notebooks with ingenious ideas for inventions, like a parachute. Engineers actually built working models of these inventions in the twentieth century.

Leonardo had many interests besides paintings, sculptures, and inventions. He was fascinated by what is inside the human body and the intricate structure of plants.

Leonardo returned to Florence in 1503. There, he painted the *Mona Lisa,* probably the most famous painting in the world.

He died in Amboise, France, in 1519, at the age of 67.

Here's what the **outline** for that article might look like with some information added from other sources.

LEONARDO DA VINCI

I. Leonardo's Jobs
  A. Painter
    1. *Mona Lisa*
    2. *The Last Supper*
  B. Sculptor
  C. Architect
  D. Military engineer
  E. Inventor
    1. Weapons
      a. Missiles
      b. Machine guns
      c. Grenades
      d. Tanks
    2. Vehicles
      a. Parachute
      b. Helicopter
      c. "Auto-Mobile"
  F. Musician
  G. Scientist

II. Early Life
  A. Born in Vinci, Italy, in 1452
  B. Florence, 1469: apprenticed to artist Andrea del Verrocchio

III. Went to work for Duke of Milan in 1482
  A. Supervised court entertainments
  B. Built military equipment
  C. Installed central heating in duke's palace
  D. Painted *The Last Supper*

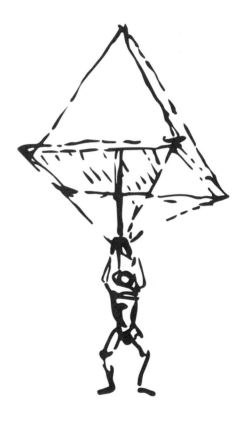

IV. **Leonardo's notebooks**
   A. Filled notebooks with ideas for inventions
   B. 20th century engineers built working models of these
      inventions
V. **Leonardo's interests**
   A. Inside the human body
   B. The structure of plants
VI. **Later life**
   A. Returned to Florence in 1503
   B. Painted the *Mona Lisa*
   C. Died in France in 1519

FIND OUT MORE ABOUT . . .

Notice that in the outline above, there aren't many details numbered
1., 2., etc., or sub-details lettered a., b., c., etc. That shows that more
facts have to be discovered before this outline is finished.

You couldn't write your whole research paper based on one
encyclopedia article and your first outline. But now you can make up
a **list** of what you have to do **more research** on:

- Leonardo's early life (his family, his education, etc.)
- What he learned from del Verrocchio
- More specifics about his work for the Duke of Milan
- What inventions were in his notebooks
- His other interests besides the human body and plants
- His work as a painter, sculptor, architect, etc.
- His most famous paintings and sculptures
- His later life

After you've made your first outline, it's time for some serious research work so you can add more details to that outline. You can't take everything in the library home, but you can take notes on what you've found out there. The next chapter will show you how.

CHAPTER 6

NOTE IT!

OR

Get It All Down

A **NOTE** is any kind of information — a fact or an idea — that you write down in a brief form to make sure you don't forget it.

NOTE CARDS

Write on **note cards** (also called index cards). They come in different sizes (3" x 5" and 4" x 6") and can be lined or unlined.

List of Sources

Make a **List of Sources**. Write down everything about your sources that you'll need later for your **bibliography** (see chapter 13):

- the title of the book, newspaper, magazine, etc.
- the title of the article in the newspaper or magazine
- the name of the author or authors
- the publisher
- the city of publication
- the copyright date

You'll find all this information on the cover and in the first few pages of a book.

Number each separate source on your List of Sources.

On the next page is a sample of a List of Sources from a research project on penguins.

Some note cards come in colors. You can use a different color for each main topic in your outline, if you have enough colors. That would be neat.

LIST OF SOURCES

1. *Penguins Are Cool Birds* by Tiger Katt. Miami: Lester Publications, 2007.

2. *Feathered Fish* by Consuela Schlepkis. Brooklyn, NY: Kleinman Books, 1941.

3. *Waddlers in Tuxedos* by David Edward. Los Angeles: Flatiron Publishing, 2002.

4. *Penguin Art* by Nej Banter. Merrick, NY: Timothy and James Publishers, 1976.

5. Interview with Dr. Renae Irving, zoology professor and penguin specialist, Penguin House, Chelsea Public Zoo, Chelsea, MA, July 19, 2007.

6. *Penguins: Birds? Fish? Little People? What?* DVD. Williams Ornithology Productions, 2006.

NOTE: These are not real books, so don't look for them in the library.

What to Put On the Note Cards

THE NUMBER OF THE SOURCE

Put down the **source number** from your List of Sources so you'll know exactly where the information on that card came from.

PAGE NUMBERS

Put down the **page numbers** of books, newspapers, and magazines to show where you got the information on that note card. That way, you'll be able to go back and double-check if you need to.

HEADINGS

Print a **heading** on the top to help you organize your cards when you're working on your outline (see chapter 5) and writing your first draft (see chapter 14).

BRIEF FACTS

Use **quick phrases** or **short sentences**, not a gazillion words. Your note cards should be shorter than the books you're reading — much shorter.

ONE MAIN IDEA ON EACH CARD

"What Monkeys Like to Eat" should not be on the same card as "Kinds of Monkeys."

PARAPHRASE

Write in **your own words**. Look away from the book, and write the information in your own words. Then look at the book again to make sure you got the facts right.

DIRECT QUOTATIONS

If you **quote someone**, copy his or her words EXACTLY, and put **quotation marks** around them. Write down the name of the person you're quoting.

BE NEAT

Write or print **very clearly** so later you'll be able to read and understand what you've written.

Sample Note Card

① Source number (from List of Sources)

② Page number

③ Heading

④ One fact per card

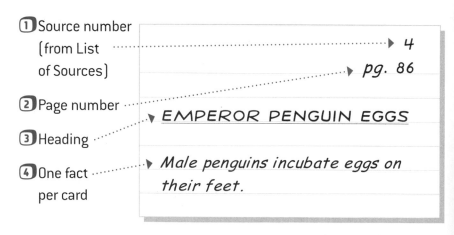

4

pg. 86

EMPEROR PENGUIN EGGS

Male penguins incubate eggs on their feet.

Photocopies

For a small fee, some libraries let you make **photocopies** of pages with maps, charts, graphs, and pictures. On the back of the photocopy, write the source and page number so you'll know where the copied pages came from. (See chapter 10 for how to use these graphics in your paper.)

You may not use all these note cards and photocopies when you write your paper, but it's better to have too much information than not enough.

TAKING NOTES ON A COMPUTER

You can also take notes on a computer. Follow the rules above. Amazingly, you might find the old-fashioned way of writing on note cards is easier than typing on a high-tech computer. Note cards are easier to sort and organize. You can write them anywhere, they weigh less than a computer, and you don't need electricity or batteries.

It may take you a few trips to the library to get all the information you need, but your note cards will be worth their weight in movie tickets once you start organizing your facts, filling in your outline, and writing your paper. Read on to see what you can find by using a computer.

CHAPTER 7

RESEARCH IT!
ON YOUR COMPUTER

OR

Research Surfing

If you have a computer, or if you can use one at school or at your local public library, you can go online and do a lot of research using a **search engine**.

WHAT IS A SEARCH ENGINE?

A **search engine** is an amazing type of computer software that searches millions of Web sites and billions of Web pages on the Internet for the information you need.

There are several free search engines **especially for kids**:

Ask for Kids
askforkids.com

Yahooligans
yahooligans.com

KidsClick!
Kidsclick.org

Looksmart
netnanny.com

Awesome Library
awesomelibrary.org

ALA Great Web Site for Kids
ala.org/greatsites

Dib Dab Doo & Dilly too
dibdabdoo.com

Fact Monster
factmonster.com

Family Source
family-source.com

FirstGov for Kids
kids.gov

Kids Search Tools
rcls.org/ksearch.htm

ThinkQuest Library
thinkquest.org/library

Google for Kids
google.com/Top/Kids_and_Teens

Some teachers limit how much of a final paper can be based on computer research, so ask.

HOW TO USE A SEARCH ENGINE

When you get onto the home page of any search engine, you'll see a blank search window at the top. On different search engines you can start looking for the information you need by

typing in keywords, names, or phrases

sneakers, Phineas Fogg, digestive system

typing in full questions

What is the life cycle of a red-eyed tree frog?

clicking on a subject category

Countries, Music, Science, Sports

Then tap your **ENTER** or **RETURN** key, or click on a screen button that says

- ● Search
- ● Ask
- ● Go
- ● Find
- ● Go Get It!

and a list of links to Web sites will magically appear.

Be Careful What You Ask For

What you type in the search window will determine how quickly you find what you're looking for among those millions of Web sites.

Basic Searches

In a basic search, you usually type in just a keyword like *nebula*, or a name like *Albert Einstein*, or a phrase like *good eating habits*.

Use Quotation Marks

To make sure the search engine looks for the words in a name or phrase all together and not separately, put quotation marks around the words: "Empire State Building," "Harry Potter," or "Spanish-American War."

To save time and avoid frustration, **narrow** your search. Be as **specific** as you can about what you ask the search engine to look for.

BILL HART, WHERE ARE YOU?

Let's say you want to find out about a little-known baseball player from the late 1800s named Bill Hart. He was supposed to be one of the worst pitchers ever to play in the major leagues.

The word *bill* can mean a restaurant bill, a duck's bill, a five-dollar bill, or a congressional bill. *Hart* means a male deer. And lots of people are named Bill or Hart or even Bill Hart.

Type **bill hart** or **Bill Hart** without quotation marks into the search window and you could find yourself on a Web site about a **bill** that a senator named **Hart** introduced in the U.S. Senate.

"Bill Hart" (with quotation marks) can lead you to Web sites about a Bill Hart who's a movie stunt man and another Bill Hart who's a guitarist.

Bill Hart pitcher will take you to a Web site about William Hart, an American silversmith of the early 1800s, who made a silver cream pitcher that is now in a museum.

You need to tell the search engine more specifically what you're seeking.

Type in **"Bill Hart" baseball pitcher** and BINGO!, the search engine will immediately offer you links to many Web sites about the very Bill Hart you want to know more about. It's as easy as that!

Narrow your search as much as possible. If you're researching "cold water tropical fish," type in all those words with quotation marks, not just *fish*.

Read what's written under each Web site link and you'll find sites to click on that might have the information you're looking for.

Click on a link and that Web site's home page will appear. Then surf away to the Web pages on that Web site!

HOW TO KNOW IF A WEB SITE IS RIGHT FOR YOU

A Web site is good when it contains the information you're looking for, written in a way that you can understand. If the Web site is from a college, museum, historical or scientific society, government agency, or any similar institution, the information on it is probably accurate. However, some Web sites may contain facts that are not so correct. If you're not sure, ask a parent, a teacher, or a librarian to look at the Web site with you.

⦿ **MAKE NOTE CARDS** when you find facts or quotes on a Web page that you'd like to use, just as if you were reading a book (see chapter 6).

⦿ **AVOID PLAGIARISM** (see chapter 12) by taking notes in your own words. Never "copy and paste" sentences or paragraphs from a Web site directly into your paper. Unless you're directly quoting someone's words and giving credit to that person (see chapter 11), always write in your own words.

If you don't find what you're seeking on one Web site, try another. Keep surfing the Web!

⦿ **CITE YOUR INTERNET SOURCES** along with all your other sources (see chapter 13).

◙ PRINT OUT ILLUSTRATIONS, CHARTS, GRAPHS, MAPS, PHOTOGRAPHS, DRAWINGS, TIME LINES, DIAGRAMS or other graphics that you can put into your paper (see chapter 10).

◙ DOWNLOAD, SAVE, AND PRINT OUT THE WEB PAGES in case you need to double-check your information. Sometimes Web sites change or are hard to find again. Your teacher may also want to see the Web pages you've gotten your information from.

ONLINE DICTIONARIES AND ENCYCLOPEDIAS

You can also find dictionaries and encyclopedias online. Most are free, but you may have to register and pay to use others at home. Some of these same Web sites may be free on a library or school computer, so ask at the library or your school. Here are some free sites to sample:

Online Dictionaries

- ◙ dictionary.com
- ◙ wordcentral.com
- ◙ onelook.com
- ◙ alphadictionary.com
- ◙ thefreedictionary.com
- ◙ yourdictionary.com

Online Encyclopedias

- encyclopedia.com
- encarta.com
- britannica.com
- reference.com

Before you use a fact you've found on a Web site in your report, try to find the same fact in at least one other source, like another Web site or a book.

Doing research on your computer is fun. You can do it at any time of the day or night, when it's snowing out, or in your pajamas with your cat on your lap. But don't forget all those wonderful **books** in your school or public library just bursting with great information about your subject.

And while you're surfing the Net and poring over books, remember that you can learn a lot from real live people, too! People who have been there and done that can share fascinating personal memories and ideas. To learn how to find and interview them, see the next chapter.

CHAPTER 8

RESEARCH IT! WITH INTERVIEWS

· · · · · · · · · · · · · · · OR · · · · · · · · · · · · · · ·

"I'd like to ask you a few questions, please."

WHY CONDUCT PERSONAL INTERVIEWS?

Because you can

- do research in a new way
- discover up-to-date knowledge not yet in books
- tap memories of events from those who were there
- learn new ideas
- be able to ask questions and get answers
- meet interesting people

Remember those irresistible words from chapter 3: "**Can you help me, please?**" Adults like helping kids with their homework. They were once kids with homework, too. They are flattered when young people are interested in their knowledge, experiences, and opinions. You may not realize it, but there are people all around you who could help you with your research.

WHO ARE THESE PEOPLE?

- relatives
- friends
- relatives of friends
- friends of relatives
- neighbors
- people in your school
- people in your town or city
- people far away

People to interview

- experts in the field you're writing about
- scientists
- explorers
- inventors
- government officials
- business leaders
- teachers
- authors
- people in stores

You can conduct an interview

- face-to-face
- by phone
- by mail
- by e-mail
- by fax

How to think of someone to interview: Ask your parents, teachers, librarian, neighbors, friends, etc., for suggestions.

The woman down the street could have fought in the Iraq War, played college basketball, grown prize-winning cucumbers, or performed brain surgery. Interview her to get great stuff for your paper.

RESEARCH TOPIC	PERSON OR PLACE TO CONTACT
History of your state	The state historian
Invention of the telephone	Someone at the local telephone company
How to raise a pig	A local farmer or 4-H Club member
How laws are made	Your state senator or representative
The war in Iraq	Someone at your local veteran's association or the US Dept. of Defense; relatives or friends' relatives who might have fought in the war
What makes songbirds sing?	An ethnological association or local Audubon Society member; local bird-watching group; natural history museum staff member; bird specialist at the local zoo
Shakespeare's greatest heroes	A high school or college English teacher or theater director; a local acting-school teacher
Why dogs make the best pets	Dog trainer; pet store owner; kennel club member; friends and relatives who own dogs; a veterinarian
What clouds are for	Weather forecasters (meteorologists) at your local radio or TV station; the science teacher at your school
A day in the life of the mayor	The mayor or someone in the mayor's office
Progress in fighting cancer	The American Cancer Society information officer; local hospital personnel; your family doctor
Were birds once dinosaurs?	Science professor at a college; dinosaur expert at a natural history museum
What a jury does	Local judge or a lawyer; someone who's been on a jury
The healthiest foods	A nutritionist; someone at the US Food and Drug Administration; the Secretary of Agriculture; the owner of a local health-food store; a healthy person
Exercises kids should do every day	Health club manager; personal trainer; your gym teacher; your pediatrician; a coach

What you should try to find out about someone you want to interview:

- Name
- Address
- Phone number
- Fax number
- E-mail address

How to find the people you want to interview:

- Ask your teachers, parents, friends, neighbors, etc.
- Look people up in the phone book.
- Use an Internet search engine to find their names, jobs, or organizations.

If a person says you can interview him or her in person, ask an adult (like a parent, relative, older sibling, etc.) to go with you. Introduce your companion to your interviewee when you get there.

What to say when you first contact a person:

- "Hello, my name is _____."
- "I'm in the ____ grade at _____ School."
- "I am writing a research paper on _____."
- "I would like to interview you on this subject."
- "I have about ____ questions, and it should take only a few minutes."
- "Can you help me, please?"

If the person says yes, then ask:

- "Would it be more convenient for you if I came to your office or home?"
- "Is it better for you if I e-mailed, faxed, or mailed you my questions?"
- "Can we have the interview by phone?"

When you contact the office of an important or busy person, you might not be able to interview that person directly, but you might be able to submit written questions, or you might be referred to someone else who can answer your questions.

What to have for a person-to-person or phone interview:

- ☑ List of questions (very important!)
- ☑ Paper, pen, pencils (you can't remember everything)
- ☑ Tape recorder and extra batteries (ask permission before you begin taping)

After the interview, send the person you interviewed a nice thank-you note or thank-you e-mail.

Before you interview someone, do some preliminary research so you'll know what to ask.

Ask questions

- about things you want to know about
- to fill in blanks in your research
- that can be answered by more than just "yes" or "no"
- that will give you answers loaded with interesting information

You can find a sample blank interview sheet on page 98.

Cite an interview in your bibliography by telling the name of the person you interviewed and where and when the interview took place (see chapter 13).

> **Interview with Joshua Lord, owner of Lord's Artistic Tattoos, El Rito, NM, July 28, 2006.**

SURVEYS AND QUESTIONNAIRES

Sometimes it's good to find out how a lot of people feel about a certain subject. The best way is to conduct a survey.

You could stand in front of the school one morning with a clipboard and ask students, "Which pets do you like better: bats or sharks?" Record the answers on a chart.

SURVEY: FAVORITE PETS			
BATS	SHARKS	OTHER	DON'T LIKE PETS
ЖЖ ЖЖ ЖЖ ЖЖ ЖЖ ЖЖ ЖЖ ЖЖ ЖЖ	ЖЖ ЖЖ ЖЖ ЖЖ ЖЖ ЖЖ ЖЖ I	II	II

Let's suppose you got 100 kids to give their opinions. Fifty-five said bats. Forty-one said sharks. One said an octopus, one said a goat, and two said they don't like pets. Then in your paper you could write:

> *In a recent survey of students at our school, 55 percent of those who responded preferred bats as pets, 41 percent preferred sharks, and 4 percent named other pets or said they didn't like pets at all.*

You can also conduct a survey by means of a questionnaire. Print copies of your questions and hand them out. Ask people to fill them in and give them back to you. Put the results in your research report.

In your bibliography, you can cite the survey or questionnaire like this (see chapter 13):

Survey (or questionnaire) of 100 students, grades 5–7, Albert Einstein Middle School, Dec. 13, 2006.

To learn about places where you can interview people and get good information for your research paper, turn to the next chapter.

QUESTIONNAIRE

WHICH PET DO YOU LIKE BETTER? (PLEASE CHECK ONE)

- ☐ BAT
- ☐ SHARK
- ☐ OTHER
- ☐ DON'T LIKE PETS

PLEASE RETURN THIS QUESTIONNAIRE TO TIMOTHY JAMES IN ROOM 5E.

THANK YOU.

CHAPTER 9

RESEARCH IT!
AT DIFFERENT PLACES

· · · · · · · · · · · · · OR · · · · · · · · · · · · ·

Have Pen, Will Travel

When you're doing your research, you don't have to stay at your library or in front of your computer. You can open the door and get out into the free, fresh air and **visit places** to gather more information.

Before you go rushing out into the streets, make sure you know where you're going. Check your local phone book or an Internet search engine for possible places nearby to visit. **Call ahead** to see what they have to offer.

You might be able to

- interview people (see chapter 8)

- see exhibits and displays (take notes, see chapter 6)

- collect free printed material (take your book bag)

If you're seeking information about . . .	You could go to . . .
Artists or works of art	Art museum
Historical events	History museum; historical society
US wars	Local veterans groups; US Dept. of Defense
Products	Factories; stores; company head-quarters
Countries, cultures, etc.	Foreign consulates; embassies; tourist/visitor information offices; travel agencies
Natural history and science	Local natural history or science museum
Diseases, medicines, treatments	Doctors' offices; pharmacies; hospitals
Animals	Zoos; vet's offices; pet stores
Plants or flowers	Botanical gardens; florists; plant stores
Lives of presidents	Presidential museums or libraries

If some of these places are not near you, you can use an Internet search engine (see chapter 7) to find out their

- Web sites or e-mail addresses
- mailing addresses or fax numbers
- toll-free phone numbers

With e-mail, toll-free calls, or some stamps, you can contact places anywhere in the world. These places often have brochures, pamphlets, and other materials that they're happy to send to you — for free! You'll be amazed at what some places will send you. Just make sure to cite any sources you use (see chapter 13).

You don't want your paper to be just words, words, words. To find out how to add colorful and interesting graphics to your report, turn to the next chapter.

CHAPTER 10

PICTURE IT!

OR

What's a Picture Worth?

A research paper doesn't have to be filled with just

words, words.

BOR-ING!

Most readers, including teachers, enjoy a report more when it has pictures in it, but ask your teacher to make sure he or she accepts them.

For many years people have been saying that **a picture is worth a thousand words**.

That doesn't mean that if your research paper has to be 2,000 words long, you can hand in just two pictures and expect to get a good grade.

NO WAY!

But it does mean that adding **graphics** to your research paper will make it more interesting and informative for your readers. And more fun to read!

Here are some graphics you could include in your paper:

- **illustrations** of the digestive and respiratory systems
- **maps** of important explorations
- **charts** of bestselling songs year by year
- **diagrams** of world-changing inventions
- **photographs** of famous people
- **drawings** of plants and flowers
- **tables** showing kids' favorite after-school activities
- **graphs** showing the number of TVs, phones, and computers in the United States
- **time lines** comparing Roman and Greek history

If you find a graphic that you think you'd like to use in your paper, ask yourself:

- "Will this picture, graph, or map help my readers better understand what I'm writing?"

- "Will it make my paper more attention-grabbing or enjoyable to read?"

- "Will it add more information to my writing?"

If the answers are YES, then go for it. Photocopy or cut out the picture (but never from library property).

For instance, it might be hard for a reader to follow the route of Lewis and Clark's 1803–1806 expedition west just by reading

> from St. Louis, Missouri, up the Mississippi River, to north of present-day Omaha, Nebraska, to near present-day Sioux City, Iowa, through South and North Dakota and the Great Plains, to the Missouri River, into Montana, over the Rocky Mountains, through Idaho, into the state of Washington, finally to the mouth of the Columbia River.

That's just **words, words, words, words, words, words, words words, words, words, words, words, words, words, words.**

Your readers will be grateful for a map and a time line that make it easy for them to visualize the journey.

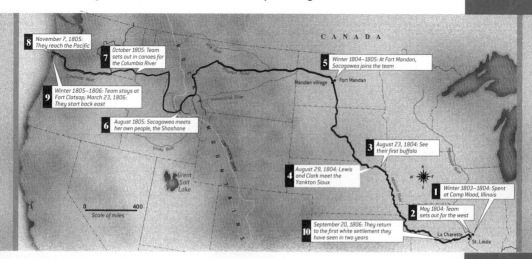

8 November 7, 1805: They reach the Pacific

7 October 1805: Team sets out in canoes for the Columbia River

5 Winter 1804–1805: At Fort Mandan, Sacagawea joins the team

CANADA

Mandan village • Fort Mandan

9 Winter 1805–1806: Team stays at Fort Clatsop; March 23, 1806: They start back east

6 August 1805: Sacagawea meets her own people, the Shoshone

3 August 23, 1804: See their first buffalo

Great Salt Lake

4 August 29, 1804: Lewis and Clark meet the Yankton Sioux

1 Winter 1803–1804: Spent at Camp Wood, Illinois

2 May 1804: Team sets out for the west

0   400
Scale of miles

10 September 20, 1806: They return to the first white settlement they have seen in two years

La Charette
St. Louis

GET MAPS, PICTURES, DRAWINGS, ETC., FROM

- books (photocopies only!)
- magazines and newspapers (ask permission before cutting them out)
- brochures and pamphlets
- Web sites
- Yourself (see next paragraph)

Feeling creative? Can't find exactly the right graphic? You can draw **your own** great illustrations, make **your own** snappy charts, graphs, and diagrams, and take **your own** beautiful photos to include in your paper.

You can glue, paste, or tape the larger pictures you've found onto paper (construction paper is colorful) and insert them into your report as separate sheets. Or you can cut out smaller illustrations and paste them onto pages with writing. Print out your writing, cut it out, then neatly arrange the pictures and writing on a page before you get out the glue.

HOW TO EXPLAIN TO YOUR READERS WHAT'S IN THE PICTURES:

- Add a title or heading above, or
- Add a caption below

Tell your readers where your illustrations came from. For example, under a diagram of the insides of an Egyptian pyramid, you could cite its source like this:

Diagram from <u>Land of the Ancient Pharaohs</u>

and then list the author, title, and publication information in your bibliography (see chapter 13).

Remember that although illustrations make a report more interesting to look at, a report is mainly about the writing. The writing counts more than the pictures. So make sure you have plenty of good writing in your paper.

Now picture this: You read something someone has said or written and you want to put it into your paper. But how can you tell a true fact from an opinion? That can sometimes be tricky. To find out how to separate the two, see the next chapter.

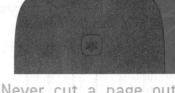

Never cut a page out of a book or library magazine or newspaper. Carefully photocopy the picture you want to use.

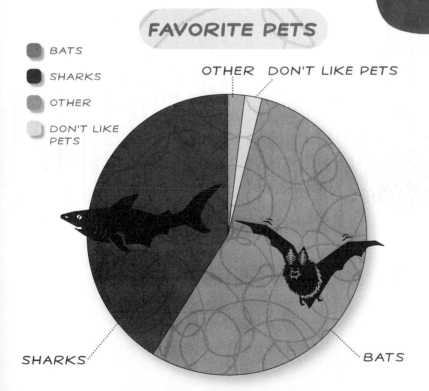

FAVORITE PETS

- BATS
- SHARKS
- OTHER
- DON'T LIKE PETS

OTHER   DON'T LIKE PETS

SHARKS

BATS

SCHOOL QUESTIONNAIRE

CHAPTER 11

SEPARATE IT!

······· OR ·······

Fact versus Opinion

A **fact** is a piece of information that you can prove to be true. It is something that really exists or really happened. A fact is real. That's a fact.

An **opinion**, on the other hand, is someone's thoughts about a subject. An opinion is a personal judgment.

Here is a **FACT** about Abraham Lincoln's beard:

> Lincoln was the first president to wear a beard.

Here is an **OPINION** about Abraham Lincoln's beard:

> *Lincoln looked better with his beard than without it.*

A person's opinion might be very real to her or him, but it's not a provable fact. It's only that person's feelings.

Here are some facts and opinions about the same subjects:

FACT: Bubble gum was invented in the United States in 1928 by Walter E. Diemer.

OPINION: *It's annoying when kids pop their bubbles.*

FACT: The Roman numeral for 1776 is MDCCLXXVI.

OPINION: *Roman numerals are fun to figure out.*

FACT: The colors of the flag of Italy are green, white, and red.

OPINION: *Those colors look nice together.*

FACT: The biggest carrot ever grown weighed almost seventeen pounds.

OPINION: *That's not so big.*

FACT: NASCAR is the fastest growing spectator sport in the United States.

OPINION: *Basketball is more exciting to watch.*

FACT: Television was invented in the 1920s.

OPINION: *Too much television can warp your brain.*

FACT: The Statue of Zeus was one of the Seven Wonders of the Ancient World.

OPINION: *The Statue of Liberty is prettier.*

If a person is important in his or her field — a great scientist, world leader, or artist — that person's opinion might be valuable to mention in your paper. But be careful not to state opinions as if they are facts.

When you state someone's opinion, you must always name the person.

DIRECT AND INDIRECT QUOTES

You can put a person's opinion into a **direct quote** (the person's exact words in quotation marks) like this:

> Dr. K. R. Youngman, a noted zoologist, said, "Walruses are the cutest animals on Earth."

You might want to use an **indirect quote** (the person's words rephrased without quotation marks) like this:

> Dr. K. R. Youngman, a noted zoologist, thinks that the cutest animals on Earth are walruses.

Sometimes the dividing line between fact and opinion is not so clear. For instance —

FACT: There's a law in Florida that says if you tie an elephant to a parking meter, you have to pay the same as you would for a car.

OPINION: *That's really weird.*

You and everybody else in the world (including elephants) might think that the Florida law is weird, but if you say it's weird, you're stating an opinion, not a fact. The law is a fact. That it's weird is an opinion.

To make sure you don't accidentally state facts and opinions as if they are your own words, read the next chapter. It tells you how to avoid plagiarism, and that's serious business.

CHAPTER 12

EXPRESS IT!
IN YOUR OWN WORDS

········· **OR** ···········

Don't Be a Wordnapper

When you start your research, you probably won't know too much about your subject. That's why you have to do the research.

One important thing that you must learn to avoid is plagiarism (**play**-juh-rizm).

When people plagiarize, they make it seem as if the words and ideas of other people are their own. The word plagiarize comes from *plagiare*, an ancient Latin verb that means "to kidnap." It sounds serious, doesn't it?

It is.

People who plagiarize are hijacking other people's words and pretending that they are theirs. They may not mean to do it, but this could actually be called stealing. Many schools have serious punishments for students who plagiarize. Some schools use special computer programs to see if students have copied sentences or paragraphs from Web sites or other people's papers.

IT'S EASY TO AVOID PLAGIARISM:

- Write as much as you can *in your own words*.

- Put **quotation marks** around someone's words when you copy them directly into your paper.

- **Cite all your sources**. Let the reader know where you got your facts, ideas, and quotes.

To find out how to cite all your sources, both fact and opinion, and avoid being a wordnapper, turn to the next chapter.

Some teachers limit the number of direct quotes in a research paper, so ask your teacher about this.

CHAPTER 13

CITE IT!

·············· **OR** ··············

Giving Credit Where Credit Is Due

As you do your research, you'll get facts and ideas from

- books
- Web sites
- magazines
- newspapers
- encyclopedias
- people you interview
- media (DVDs, CDs, films, videos, etc.)
- places you've visited or contacted

In your paper, you have to tell your readers where you got your information. This is called **citing your sources**. Use the List of Sources you compiled while doing your research (see chapter 6).

WITHIN YOUR PAPER YOU DO THIS WITH

- **footnotes** at the bottom of each page, or
- **endnotes** at the end of the paper, or
- **source notes** after some sentences in your paper

AT THE END OF YOUR PAPER YOU

- put all your sources into the **bibliography** (see page 75).

WHEN TO CITE YOUR SOURCES

It's not necessary to cite every statement in your paper. For instance, you don't have to cite facts that everybody already knows are true, like

- the Earth is a planet
- dogs bark
- water is wet

Just cite the new facts that you learned while doing your research so your readers will know where you got them.

FOOTNOTES, ENDNOTES, SOURCE NOTES

Footnotes

A **footnote** is a note at the **bottom** (foot) of a page that tells where you found a piece of specific information or a quote that's on that page.

Ask your teacher which kind of citing to use: footnotes, endnotes, or source notes.

Make sure to leave room at the bottom of each page for the footnotes for that page. Most computer word-processing applications have autoformatting programs that can do that for you.

Put a **raised number** (called a superscript) half a space above the last word in the sentence you're citing the source for.

In 1893, the Supreme Court of the United States officially declared that the tomato is a vegetable, even though by strict definition, it's a fruit.[1]

At the **bottom of the page**, put the **same raised number** and give information like that in the bibliography. The format of a footnote is slightly different from that in your bibliography (see example below).

[1] Blanca Millan, <u>Fruits vs. Vegetables: What's What?</u> (New York: Manny Books, 2005), 17.

Footnotes are numbered 1, 2, 3, etc.

Endnotes

When you put all your footnotes together **after the last page of your writing** (before the bibliography) they're called **endnotes**. Endnotes are easier to do than footnotes because you don't have to be careful about leaving space for them at the bottom of each page.

Source Notes

The easiest way to cite sources is with source notes.

A source note contains just

- the author's **last name**
- the **number of the page** where you found the information

Everything else about that book will be in the bibliography.

A source note comes

- **right after** the information you're citing
- **before the period** at the end of the sentence

A source note is always in **parentheses**.

> William Shakespeare was an actor as well as a playwright and may have performed the part of the ghost in the very first production of his play *Hamlet* (Timothy, 32).

BIBLIOGRAPHY

A **bibliography** is the **last thing** in your research paper. It's a list that shows where you got all your information.

There is a special way to arrange most entries in a bibliography:

- alphabetical order by the author's last name (or the name of the periodical, film, or person interviewed)
- indent all lines after the first in each entry

Sources

You must always give five main pieces of information about any source you use. You should find what you need on your List of Sources (see chapter 6).

1. the author or authors
2. the title of the book, article, or Web site
3. where it was published
4. who published it
5. when it was published (or when you found it on a Web site)

For books, the copyright date is the date the book was published. Look for this symbol: ©.

You will find this information on the title page and the copyright page right at the beginning of the book.

NOTE: The books in the examples below are made up, but the punctuation is the way it should be.

Ask your teacher if he or she wants you to include the page numbers you found your facts on.

Titles of books and periodicals can be either **underlined** (Hero Chickens of Alaska) or typed in **italics** (*Hero Chickens of Alaska*).

BOOKS WITH ONE AUTHOR

Author's last name, Author's first name.
Title of book. City of publication: Name of publisher, Year of Publication.

Kilmer, Sue. What Goes On in the Principal's Office.
Pine Plain, NY: Columbia Books, 2005.

BOOKS WITH TWO OR THREE AUTHORS

First author's last name, first author's first name, and next author's or authors' first and last names, Title of book. City of publication: Name of publisher, Year of publication.

Two authors

Greenblatt, Irwin, and Audrey Wishneff, Rosy Future: Retired in New York. Philadelphia: Maya Books, 2007.

Three authors

Gerson, Al, Lorrie Howard, and Adam Leslie, City Dwellers.
Hemlock Farms, PA: Granite Publishing, 1978.

BOOKS WITH MORE THAN THREE AUTHORS

First author's last name, first author's first name, et al. <u>Title of book</u>. City of publication: Name of publisher, Year of publication.
Note: *et al.* is Latin for "and others."

Penn, Roslyn, et al. <u>The Hippest Senior</u>. Lynn, MA: Jade Publications, 1997.

MAGAZINE ARTICLES

Author's last name, Author's first name. "Title of article." <u>Name of magazine</u>. Volume number (if any). Date of publication: Page number(s).

Rachel, Jennifer. "How to Make Fabulous Jewelry." <u>American Gems</u>. Vol.30./July 19, 1976: 66-99.

ENCYCLOPEDIAS

Author of Article (last name first, if given). "Title of article." <u>Title of Book</u>. Volume number and edition, if given. City of Publication: Publisher, Year.

Robert, George. "Pharmacies of the Middle Ages. " <u>Hawthorne Encyclopedia</u>. Vol. 6. Third Edition. Chelsea, MA; Glonnie Books, 2001.

NEWSPAPER ARTICLES

Author's last name, Author's first name. "Title of article." <u>Name of newspaper</u>. Date of publication, Section and page number.

Freedman, Loraine. "Girls of the Bible." <u>The Peabody Bugle</u>. July 22, 2006, J 20.

PERSONAL INTERVIEWS

Last name of person interviewed, First name of person
interviewed. Personal Interview. Location where interview took
place. Date of interview.

Soghoian, Richard. Personal interview. Columbia Prep School,
New York. Aug. 3, 2005.

SURVEYS AND QUESTIONNAIRES

Survey (or questionnaire) of the number of people who were
questioned, where the survey took place or the questions that
were asked, the date of the survey or questionnaire.

Survey (or questionnaire) of 75 shoppers, MegaMall, Peabody,
MA, June 22, 2006.

WEB SITES

When you use information that you found on a Web site (see chapter
7), try to give as much information about it in your bibliography as
you can. Put angle brackets (< >) around the Internet address. Since
Web sites can change without notice, it's always a good idea to print
out pages and save them so that you or your teacher can refer to
them again.

Web Sites with an Author's Name

Author's last name (if given), Author's first name (if given) .
"Title of article or page." Internet: < Internet address> Date
you got the information.

Cohen, Sandee. "General Ransom: A Hero's Life." Internet:
<http://www.loomisatrh.com> April 8, 2006.

Web Sites with No Author's Name

Sometimes the Web site doesn't tell you who wrote what you're quoting. In that case, you could cite that Web site like this:

"Title of article or page." Internet: <Internet address> Date you got the information.

"Prep School Programs of Study." Internet: <http://cgps.org> Dec. 6, 2005.

COMPUTER SOFTWARE (CD-ROMS, DISKS, ETC.)

Author's last name (if given), Author's first name (if given). Title of software. Computer software. Name of publisher, Copyright date or date of publication. Type of software (CD-ROM, disk, etc.).

Gylanders, Jed. The Flying London Cabby. Computer software. Luxborough Media, 2003. CD-ROM.

TELEVISION SHOWS

Name of network. Name of series. "Name of episode." Date, time of broadcast.

Life Stories Channel. People Who Care. "Lisa: The Brave School Nurse." April 1, 2006, 2:00 P.M. to 3:00 A.M.

FILMS (SEEN IN THEATERS, ON TV, DVDS, OR VIDEOTAPE)

Title of Film. Film. Videotape. DVD. Name of studio or production company. Year of production.

Global Girl. DVD. Monica M. Cinema. 2004.

OTHER MATERIALS

If you've used information from brochures or pamphlets that you got from companies or agencies (see chapter 9), you could cite these sources like this:

"How to Teach Your Parrot to Sing Opera," Booklet. The Society for
   Performing Animals. 1994.

Now that you've done your research, written your note cards, and cited your sources, it's time to begin writing your paper. The end is in sight! So go to the next page, and find out what to do to move this thing along to its conclusion.

CHAPTER 14

WRITE IT!

········· OR ·············

Follow Your Outline

When you've completed all your research, it's time to set aside a good chunk of quiet time and get your paper written. You're nearing the finish line. You're ready to write your **first draft**.

The hardest part—doing the research—is over. The rest should go smoothly.

Hang a "Do Not Disturb" sign on your door (there's one for you on page 94).

Remember that "journey of a thousand miles" you started in chapter 1? Well, you've traveled about 953 miles already. Only a few more to go.

Clear your desk or table.

Gather up

- your finished outline
- all your note cards
- your List of Sources
- surveys and questionnaires
- interview papers
- photocopies
- pictures you've printed from your computer
- anything else that you found in your research

You could work on your first draft, on and off, a little each day, for a few days.

Loosen up your fingers, get some paper and a pen, or turn on your computer. Let's write this report!

Here's an easy, step-by-step guide to get you going:

Organize Your Paper

There are different ways to organize a paper once you've done all your research. On the following two pages are four of the most common:

① TIME ORDER (usually from beginning to end or earliest to latest)

The Life Cycle of a Butterfly

I. Adult butterfly lays egg
II. Egg hatches into caterpillar or larva
III. Caterpillar forms chrysalis or pupa
IV. Chrysalis grows into a butterfly
V. Butterfly comes out

② ORDER OF IMPORTANCE (from most to least important or least to most important)

Reasons Not to Smoke

I. Makes your breath smell bad
II. Stinks up your clothes, hair, etc.
III. Can cause cigarette burns on clothes and furniture
IV. Stains teeth and fingers
V. Causes wrinkles
VI. Causes disagreements with people who don't want you to smoke
VII. Costs a lot of money
VIII. Can cause gum disease
IX. Can cause coughs and sore throats
X. Can cause fires
XI. Increases risk of heart disease and lung cancer

③ CAUSE AND EFFECT

What Causes Thunderstorms?

I. Moisture in lower to mid levels of atmosphere
II. Unstable air that keeps rising
III. A lifting force that makes the air rise

④ COMPARE AND CONTRAST

Show how two or more subjects are alike (compare) or different (contrast).

Abraham Lincoln and John F. Kennedy

I. How They Were Alike

   A. Elections

      1. Lincoln elected congressman in 1846; president in 1860

      2. Kennedy elected congressman in 1946; president in 1960

   B. Deaths

      1. Lincoln assassinated by gun on a Friday

      2. Kennedy assassinated by gun on a Friday

II. How They Were Different

   A. Elections

      1. Lincoln lost most elections he ran in

      2. Kennedy won every election he ran in

   B. Re-elections

      1. Lincoln was re-elected president, then killed

      2. Kennedy was killed before he could be re-elected

Get Your Writing Started

▪ Begin with the **FIRST MAJOR TOPIC** on your outline.

   ▪ Read the note cards that relate <u>just to that topic</u>.

   ▪ Write the first paragraph in your own words. (The first paragraph should introduce the topic.)

      • Use **complete sentences**.

      • Add in the **subtopics** and **details**.

      • Double-check for **accuracy**.

      • Put **quotation marks** around direct quotes.

      • **Cite your sources** as you go along.

Make sure that your details support your subtopics and your

subtopics support your main topic. As you write, try to make your paper as interesting and informative as possible.

Pause. That wasn't so bad, was it?

- Read over what you've just written. Make corrections.
- Now, repeat this process with the **SECOND MAJOR TOPIC** on your outline.

Continue this way, topic by topic, detail by detail, until you get tired.

Put away what you've written so far. Start again when you feel refreshed.

When you begin again, read over what you've already written. Make any changes and corrections. Then, move on to the next major topic.

Before you know it, you'll come to the last sub-detail on your outline and your last note card.

Your first rough draft is done! Take a break. You deserve it.

OK. Break's over. Now come the last things to do: Write your **final copy**, put it all together, and hand it in. Read the next and last chapter for that.

See chapter 13 for tips on footnotes, endnotes, and source notes.

Leave room for changes, additions, and corrections. If you're typing, double space. If you're writing your paper by hand, leave every other line blank.

WHEW!

CHAPTER 15

REVISE IT!

······· OR ·············

Saving the Best for Last

You're coming to the final mile in your journey of a thousand miles. The signpost is just up ahead: DONE! You've finished practically all of the work already. But the last part is very important. You have to **get your research paper ready to hand in** to your teacher.

REWRITING

All good writers know that the most important part of writing is rewriting. Now's the time to remember all those writing skills you've been learning in school: spelling, punctuation, capitalization, sentence structure, paragraphing, etc.

Read over your rough draft. With a colored pen or pencil, make changes, corrections, and revisions in the margins and blank spaces.

TEACHER'S REQUIREMENTS

Make sure you know your teacher's special rules for the paper, especially if it should be

- handwritten or typed
- single- or double-spaced
- single- or double-sided

FINAL COPY

Now, write your final copy. Use a dictionary or spell-check to make sure you find and correct all those pesky little spelling mistakes before your teacher does. Don't rush this part of the job. Go slowly and carefully.

CITE YOUR SOURCES

Remember to insert the source notes or to leave room at the bottom of each page for footnotes if that's what your teacher wants you to do. Write out your bibliography (see chapter 13). Make sure to arrange the listings in alphabetical order (usually by the authors' last names).

BE NEAT

Nobody wants to read a messy, illegible paper. Yuck!

PROOFREAD, PROOFREAD, PROOFREAD

Read your paper over slowly and carefully. Ask a parent, older sibling, or friend to read your paper, too. Be on the lookout for spelling mistakes, sentences that don't make sense, or other writing errors. Your teacher will find them if you don't. Correct them.

ADD IN THE GRAPHICS

Leave room for the graphics you've assembled (see chapter 10). Either paste them into pages with writing, or put them on separate pages by themselves. You can also "copy & paste" or save and insert them from Web sites on the Internet. Put a heading at the top or a caption at the bottom of each graphic to explain what the picture, illustration, drawing, chart, graph, or diagram shows.

TITLE

There's no strict rule about how you should choose a title for your paper. One way is to make up

- a title that catches the reader's interest
- a subtitle that tells what the research report is about

Here are some samples:

> **THE INCREDIBLE BLACKWELL WOMEN**
> America's First Female Doctor and Her Sisters

> **LAND OF 3,000 ISLANDS**
> All About Japan

> **GOOD-BYE, EARTH!**
> Yuri Gagarin, the First Person in Space

COVER

Make an eye-catching cover with the title and subtitle in big letters. Add a picture or drawing. Use colored construction paper or cardboard. Color in the letters or graphics with markers, crayons, or colored pencils.

FINAL CHECKLIST

Before you put all the pages together, give your report a serious look over. Double-check the following:

- ☑ Are all the pages as neat as I can make them?
- ☑ Have I triple-checked my spelling?
- ☑ Have I numbered all the pages neatly in the same place?
- ☑ Are all the pages in the right order?
- ☑ Do all my graphics have headings or captions?
- ☑ Have I cited all my sources?
- ☑ Does my bibliography follow the rules?
- ☑ Am I going to be proud to hand this in?

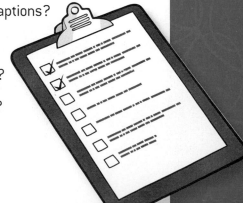

PUT IT TOGETHER

Bind the whole package with staples, tape, paper fasteners, or yarn. You could also put your report into a loose-leaf notebook or a special report folder from a stationery store. Now, give it one last look to check that everything's as perfect as you can make it.

KEEP IT SAFE

Protect it from damage by bad weather or pets. Put it into a rainproof plastic bag or a large, dirt-proof envelope.

THIS IS IT

Take it to school and HAND IT IN!
You've traveled your thousand miles.
You've **researched** it!
You've **written** it!
You're **DONE**!

CONGRATULATIONS!

Here are lots of pages to help you organize the job and get it done fast!

See chapter 1, page 12, to learn how to fill in the chart below.

TIME BUDGET CHART

Choose Your Topic		days
Write Your First Outline		days
Find Your Sources		days
Take Your Notes		days
Organize Your Facts; Finish Your Outline		days
Write Your First Draft		days
Proofread; Revise		days
Write Your Final Draft; Proofread and Correct It		days
Put It Together; Check It Over		days
Hand It In		seconds

EXTRAS

RESEARCH CALENDAR

In the blank two-month calendar below, fill in the name of the months, the dates, and your research schedule. To see a sample Research Calendar, go to page 13.

MONTH:

SUN	MON	TUES	WED	THURS	FRI	SAT

MONTH:

SUN	MON	TUES	WED	THURS	FRI	SAT
◯	◯	◯	◯	◯	◯	◯
◯	◯	◯	◯	◯	◯	◯
◯	◯	◯	◯	◯	◯	◯
◯	◯	◯	◯	◯	◯	◯
◯	◯	◯	◯	◯	◯	◯

Copy this sign and hang it on your door.

PLEASE

DO NOT

DISTURB!

RESEARCH GENIUS AT WORK
WRITING A GREAT REPORT
THANK YOU

To learn how to take notes, see chapter 6.

SAMPLE NOTE CARD

1️⃣ Source number
(from List of Sources, see page 41)

2️⃣ Page number

3️⃣ Heading

4️⃣ One fact per card

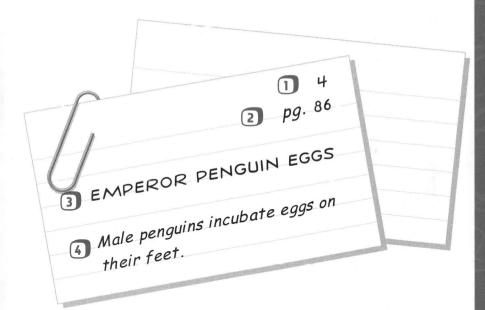

1️⃣ 4
2️⃣ pg. 86
3️⃣ EMPEROR PENGUIN EGGS
4️⃣ Male penguins incubate eggs on their feet.

SEARCH ENGINES

Here is a list of free search engines for kids. (For more about doing research with your computer using search engines, see chapter 7.)

Ask for Kids
askforkids.com

Yahooligans
yahooligans.com

KidsClick!
Kidsclick.org

Looksmart
search.netnanny.com

Awesome Library
awesomelibrary.org

ALA Great Web Sites for Kids
ala.org/greatsites

Dib Dab Doo & Dilly too
dibdabdoo.com

Fact Monster
factmonster.com

Family Source
family-source.com

FirstGov for Kids
kids.gov

Kid's Search Tools
rcls.org/ksearch.htm

ThinkQuest Library
thinkquest.org/library

Google for Kids
google.com/Top/Kids_and_Teens

ONLINE DICTIONARIES

- dictionary.com
- wordcentral.com
- onelook.com
- alphadictionary.com
- thefreedictionary.com
- yourdictionary.com

ONLINE ENCYCLOPEDIAS

- encyclopedia.com
- encarta.com
- britannica.com
- reference.com

For more about online dictionaries and encyclopedias, see chapter 7.

SAMPLE INTERVIEW SHEET

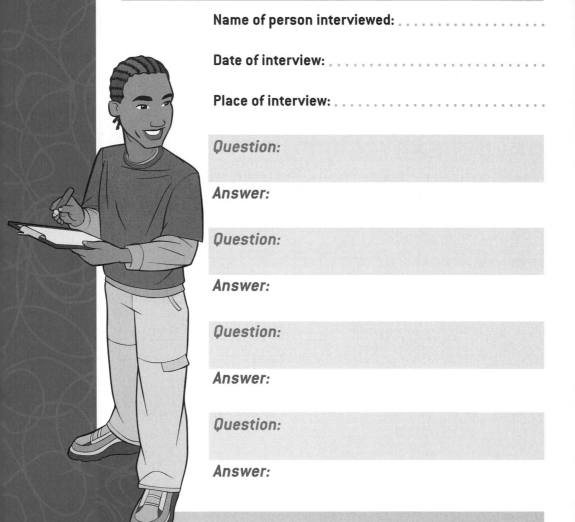

Name of person interviewed: . . . .

Date of interview: . . . .

Place of interview: . . . .

Question:

Answer:

Question:

Answer:

Question:

Answer:

Question:

Answer:

Fill in as many questions as you can think of before the interview. Leave blank spaces for questions you think up on the spot. For more about personal interviews, see chapter 8.

SAMPLE SURVEY FORM

SURVEY QUESTION:				
Choice 1	**Choice 2**	**Choice 3**	**Choice 4**	**Choice 5**
Number of people who selected that choice:				

To record how many people selected each choice, make lines like this:

⌗ ll, etc.

To learn more about how to conduct a survey, see chapter 8.

SAMPLE QUESTIONNAIRE FORM

QUESTIONNAIRE

I am doing a research report on _____,
and I would like to include your opinion. Please put a check mark in
the box next to the statement that you most agree with. Thank you.

☐ **Statement 1**

· ·

☐ **Statement 2**

· ·

☐ **Statement 3**

· ·

☐ **Statement 4**

· ·

Please return this questionnaire to_____

in room _____, or fill it out now and hand it right back to me.

Thank you for your help.

FACT VERSUS OPINION GAME

Read chapter 11 to find out how to separate fact from opinion. Then play this game with your friends to sharpen your fact-versus-opinion detection skills. The rules below are for two players, but you can easily adapt them for more than two.

1. Use any dictionary, encyclopedia, or almanac to get the facts.

2. Each player should make up his or her own opinions based on those facts.

3. Each player should write these facts and opinions on separate note cards, one fact or one opinion to a card.

4. Each player should shuffle his or her cards and give them to the other player.

5. The players should alternate reading aloud one card and stating if it is a "fact" or an "opinion." If the player is right, he or she gets one point. If the player is wrong, one point is deducted from his or her score (see score sheet on page 104).

6. At the end, the player with the most points wins.

SAMPLE "FACT" AND "OPINION" CARDS

THE DEADLIEST EARTH-QUAKE ON RECORD KILLED OVER 800,000 PEOPLE AND TOOK PLACE IN SHANXI, CHINA, IN 1556.

AN EARTHQUAKE CAN BE A LOT OF FUN WHEN THE HOUSE STARTS RATTLING AND THE DISHES START FLYING OFF THE SHELVES.

ALFRED NOBEL INVENTED DYNAMITE IN SWEDEN IN 1867.

DYNAMITE SHOULD BE BANNED BECAUSE IT CAN CAUSE SERIOUS DAMAGE IF USED INCORRECTLY.

"CONSUME," "DEVOUR," "FEAST," AND "NIBBLE" ARE ALL SYNONYMS FOR "EAT."

EATING, CONSUMING, DEVOURING, FEASTING, OR NIBBLING ON CHOCOLATE-COVERED FRENCH FRIES IS THE BEST WAY TO SNACK.

A SEQUOIA IS A GIANT EVERGREEN TREE THAT CAN GROW TO OVER 300 FEET TALL.

SEQUOIAS ARE NICE TREES, BUT ELM TREES ARE MUCH BETTER BECAUSE THEY'RE EASIER TO GROW IN YOUR BACKYARD.

A TOURIST CAN GET THE MOST DELICIOUS PIZZAS IN THE WORLD IN ITALY.

THE OFFICIAL NAME OF THE COUNTRY OF ITALY IS "REPUBBLICA ITALIANA."

"FACT VERSUS OPINION" GAME SCORE SHEET

(Use this method of scoring: ~~IIII~~ II)

NAME OF PLAYER	NUMBER OF POINTS WON	NUMBER OF POINTS LOST	FINAL SCORE (Points won minus points lost)

A SAMPLE RESEARCH REPORT
ABOUT AUSTRALIA

To show you how to put the parts of a research project together to produce a finished report, here are

- a sample List of Sources
- some sample note cards
- parts of an outline made from those note cards
- part of a research report made from that outline using source notes, endnotes, and footnotes.

NOTE: The sources and bibliography are made up, but the facts about Australia are real.

LIST OF SOURCES
for research report on Australia

1. *Island Country* by Jesse Angel. New York: Gy Landers, Inc., 2007.

2. "Come to Australia" by Barrie Allen. Internet: *http://www.SydneyTouristBoard.au* April 28, 2006.

3. *Pacific Nation* by Arnold Feinblatt. Denver: Arlene Books, 2005.

4. "Australia: Land of Beauty" by Maggie Konikowski. *Travel Lover's Magazine.* August, 2006: pages 16-19.

5. *Life Down Under* by Jayne Connell. New York: Redman Publications, 2003.

6. *People and Places* by Margo Potter. Danvers, MA: Max & Bill Books, 2006.

7. *Down and Under* by Maria Soares. New York: Maps Galore, Inc., 2001.

NOTE CARDS ON AUSTRALIA

used to make the outline on page 109

1 Source number (from List of Sources, see page 105)

2 Page number

3 Heading

4 One fact
per card

---

1 6
2 pg. 86

3 QUOTE FROM AUSTRALIAN

4 "I love living on the world's smallest continent that's also the world's largest island that's also my country."
-- Hannah C. Castell, Melbourne, Aus.

---

1 4
2 pg. 17

3 LANDSCAPE

4 Landscape: Mostly
low-lying

---

1 5
2 pg. 124

3 TROPICAL RAIN FORESTS

4 In northeast Aus. there
are many tropical rain forests

1 2
2 web page

3 TROPICAL RAIN FORESTS

4 Cover only 1% of
   the continent

1 7
2 pg. 136

3 TROPICAL RAIN FORESTS

4 Wettest parts get 296 in.
   rainfall per year

1 6
2 pg. 99

3 WHERE PEOPLE LIVE

4 Mountain range in east; most people
   live in cities east of this mount. range

1 3
2 pg. 187

3 HOTTEST/COOLEST
   MONTHS

4 Coolest: July & Aug.
   Hottest: Jan. (see Outback)

(1) 5
(2) pg. 66

(3) TEMPERATURES
IN NORTH

(4) Warm to hot
all year-round

---

(1) 1
(2) pg. 116

(3) TEMPS IN COASTAL AREAS
AROUND SYDNEY

(4) Mild in winter (50s-60s)
Warmer in summer (80s)

---

(1) 5
(2) pg. 66

(3) RAINY SEASON IN NORTH

(4) Summer: Rainy
season

---

(1) 7
(2) pg. 86

(3) THE OUTBACK

(4) Hot, dry interior; summer
temp over 100°F

---

(1) 1
(2) pg. 7

(3) HIGHER ELEVATIONS

(4) The states of Tasmania and Victoria
VERY COLD: Lot of snow and temps
below freezing

PART OF AN OUTLINE
made from the note cards on pages 106-108

I. Landscape
- A. Mostly low-lying
- B. Tropical rain forests in northeast
  - 1. Cover only 1 percent of continent
  - 2. Wettest parts receive 296 inches of rainfall a year
- C. Mountain range in east
- D. Most people live in cities east of mountain range

II. Climate
- A. Hottest/coolest months
  - 1. July and August are coolest months
  - 2. January is hottest month
- B. Coastal areas around Sydney
  - 1. Mild in winter (50s to 60s)
  - 2. Summers are warmer (in the 80s)
- C. North Australia
  - 1. Warm to hot all year
  - 2. Summer is rainy season
- D. The Outback
  - 1. Hot, dry interior of Australia
  - 2. Summer temperature over 100 degrees
- E. Higher elevations (Tasmania and Victoria)
  - 1. Lot of snow
  - 2. Temperatures are below freezing

PART OF THE FINISHED RESEARCH REPORT WITH SOURCE NOTES

made from the outline on page 109

AUSTRALIA: THE LAND DOWN UNDER
Continent, Island, Country

"I love living on the world's smallest continent that's also the world's largest island that's also my country," says Hannah C. Castell, a resident of Melbourne, Australia (Potter, 86). Ms. Castell's homeland is a fascinating and varied place to live.

The landscape of Australia is mostly low-lying (Konikowski, 17), with tropical rain forests in the northeast (Connell, 124). The rain forests take up only 1 percent of Australia's land (Allen, 325), but they are very rainy. Up to 296 inches of rain can fall there in just one year (Soares, 136). There is a mountain range in the east, and most people in Australia live in cities east of this mountain range (Potter, 99).

January and February are the hottest months; July is the coolest month (Feinblatt, 187).

The coastal areas around Sydney are usually mild (from the 50s to the 60s) in the winter and warmer (in the 80s) in the summer (Angel, 116). It is warm to hot all year-round in the north, and summer is the rainy season there (Connell, 66). In Australia's hot, dry interior, called the Outback, temperatures can soar to over 100 degrees (Soares, 86). On the other hand, in the higher elevations around Tasmania and Victoria, there is a lot of snow and the temperatures are below freezing (Angel, 7).

PART OF THE FINISHED RESEARCH REPORT WITH ENDNOTES

made from the outline on page 109

AUSTRALIA: THE LAND DOWN UNDER
Continent, Island, Country

"I love living on the world's smallest continent that's also the world's largest island that's also my country," says Hannah C. Castell, a resident of Melbourne, Australia.[1] Ms. Castell's homeland is a fascinating and varied place to live.

The landscape of Australia is mostly low-lying[2] with tropical rain forests in the northeast.[3] The rain forests take up only 1 percent of Australia's land,[4] but they are very rainy. Up to 296 inches of rain can fall there in just one year.[5] There is a mountain range in the east, and most people in Australia live in cities east of this mountain range.[6]

January and February are the hottest months; July is the coolest month.[7]

The coastal areas around Sydney are usually mild (from the 50s to the 60s) in the winter and warmer (in the 80s) in the summer.[8] It is warm to hot all year-round in the north, and summer is the rainy season there.[9] In Australia's hot, dry interior, called The Outback, temperatures can soar to over 100 degrees.[10] On the other hand, in the higher elevations around Tasmania and Victoria, there is a lot of snow and the temperatures are below freezing.[11]

[1] Margo Potter, <u>People and Places</u> (Danvers, MA: Max & Bill Books, 2006) 86.

[2] Maggie Konikowski, "Australia: Land of Beauty" (<u>Travel Lover's Magazine</u>. August, 2006) 17.

[3] Jayne Connell, <u>Life Down Under</u> (New York: Redman Publications, 2003) 124.

[4] Barrie Allen, "Come to Australia" (Internet: <<u>http://www.Sydney TouristBoard.au</u>>, 2006).

[5] Maria Soares, <u>Down and Under</u> (New York: Maps Galore, Inc., 2001) 136.

[6] Potter, 99.

[7] Arnold Feinblatt, <u>Pacific Nation</u> (Denver: Arlene Books, 2005) 187.

[8] Jesse Angel, <u>Island Country</u> (New York: Gy Landers, Inc., 2007) 116.

[9] Connell, 66.

[10] Soares, 86.

[11] Angel, 7.

Remember, endnotes go after your last page of writing, before the bibliography.

PART OF THE FINISHED RESEARCH REPORT WITH FOOTNOTES

made from the outline on page 109

AUSTRALIA: THE LAND DOWN UNDER
Continent, Island, Country

"I love living on the world's smallest continent that's also the world's largest island that's also my country," says Hannah C. Castell, a resident of Melbourne, Australia.[1] Ms. Castell's homeland is a fascinating and varied place to live.

The landscape of Australia is mostly low-lying[2] with tropical rain forests in the northeast.[3] The rain forests take up only 1 percent of Australia's land,[4] but they are very rainy. Up to 296 inches of rain can fall there in just one year.[5] There is a mountain range in the east, and most people in Australia live in cities east of this mountain range.[6]

---

[1] Margo Potter, <u>People and Places</u> (Danvers, MA: Max & Bill Books, 2006) 86.

[2] Maggie Konikowski, "Australia: Land of Beauty" (<u>Travel Lover's Magazine</u>. August, 2006) 17.

[3] Jayne Connell, <u>Life Down Under</u> (New York: Redman Publications, 2003) 124.

[4] Barrie Allen, "Come to Australia" (Internet: <<u>http://www.Sydney</u> <u>TouristBoard.au</u>>, 2006).

[5] Maria Soares, <u>Down and Under</u> (New York: Maps Galore, Inc., 2001) 136.

[6] Potter, 99.

January and February are the hottest months; July is the coolest month.[7]

The coastal areas around Sydney are usually mild (from the 50s to the 60s) in the winter and warmer (in the 80s) in the summer.[8] It is warm to hot all year-round in the north, and summer is the rainy season there.[9] In Australia's hot, dry interior, called the Outback, temperatures can soar to over 100 degrees.[10] On the other hand, in the higher elevations around Tasmania and Victoria, there is a lot of snow and the temperatures are below freezing.[11]

---

[7] Arnold Feinblatt, Pacific Nation (Denver: Arlene Books, 2005) 187.

[8] Jesse Angel, Island Country (New York: Gy Landers, Inc., 2007) 116.

[9] Connell, 66.

[10] Soares, 86.

[11] Angel, 7.

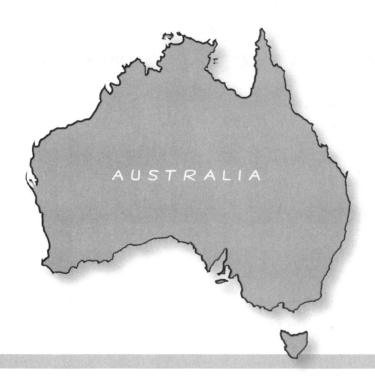

PART OF THE BIBLIOGRAPHY

Allen, Barrie. "Come to Australia." Internet: <http://www.Sydney TouristBoard.au> April 28, 2006.

Angel, Jesse. Island Country. New York: Gy Landers, Inc., 2007.

Connell, Jayne. Life Down Under. New York: Redman Publications, 2003.

Feinblatt, Arnold. Pacific Nation. Denver: Arlene Books, 2005.

Konikowski, Maggie. "Australia: Land of Beauty." Travel Lover's Magazine. August, 2006: 16-19.

Potter, Margo. People and Places. Danvers, MA: Max & Bill Books, 2006.

Soares, Maria. Down and Under. New York: Maps Galore, Inc., 2001.

A GLOSSARY OF RESEARCH TERMS

almanac
a reference book published every year that contains up-to-date tables, charts, statistics, brief articles, and lists of information on many different subjects

atlas
a reference book of maps, charts, tables, and illustrations on a particular subject like geography of the world, the anatomy of the body, etc.

bibliography
a list, usually at the end of a book or report, that gives important facts about the sources of information in that book or report (titles of books, magazines, newspapers, etc.; authors; publishers, etc.)

biographical dictionary
a reference book that contains brief articles about the lives of important people, usually arranged in alphabetical order by the person's last name

card catalog
a catalog of cards in a library that helps a researcher (you!) find a book or other research material by its author, title, or subject matter

citing sources
giving facts about all the books, magazines, newspapers, etc., in which you found the information you used to write your research report

Dewey Decimal System
a system that libraries use to classify books and other publications by subject, by giving numbers and decimals to the materials

dictionary
a reference book that contains an alphabetical list of words, with their parts of speech, pronunciations, definitions, etc.

direct quote
the exact words that a person has said or written, usually enclosed by quotation marks

electronic database
information about books, authors, titles, etc., that you search on a computer in a library

encyclopedia
a reference book or set of books that contains information on all branches of knowledge in articles, usually arranged alphabetically by subject

endnote
a note at the end of a book or paper that cites a source reference (usually author and page number)

footnote
a note at the bottom of a page that cites a source reference (usually author and page number)

graphics
pictures, drawings, illustrations, charts, graphs, photographs, and diagrams that help clarify, explain, show an example, or accompany printed text

indirect quote
the thoughts or ideas of a person expressed without using the person's exact words and not enclosed in quotation marks

Internet

a communications network that electronically interconnects computer networks from around the world

list of sources

a list of all the sources from which a researcher (you!) got his or her information

media center

a library that contains multimedia resources like films, DVDs, CD-ROMs, CDs, etc., in addition to books

microfiche

a sheet of microfilm containing rows of tiny images of pages of printed matter, especially newspapers

microfilm

a film with small pictures of printed or other material

note card

an index card on which a researcher (you!) writes down the information he or she has gotten from books, magazines, newspapers, and other sources

outline

an organized draft or plan that briefly summarizes the important information about a subject in order of importance using headings, subheadings, etc.

periodicals

newspapers, magazines, newsletters, and similar material that is published at regular periods of time (every day, every week, every month, etc.)

plagiarism

making it seem as if someone else's words or ideas are your own without giving credit to the true source

quotation book

a reference book that gives quotes made by notable people (statesmen, artists, inventors, authors, etc.) on many different subjects, organized either by the name of the person who made the quote or by the subject matter

research

the careful, studious, and diligent search for information about a particular subject

search engine

computer software used to search for information on the Internet

source

the book, newspaper, magazine, person, CD-ROM, Web site, etc., from which a researcher (you!) gets his or her information about a subject

source note

a note placed at the end of a sentence to cite a source reference (author and page number, enclosed in parentheses)

thesaurus

a reference book of words and their synonyms (and sometimes their antonyms)

Web site

a group of Web pages and a home page put onto the Internet by a person, a company, a school, the government, or any organization

World Wide Web (also known as www)

part of the Internet that contains millions of Web sites that a researcher (you!) can access on a computer

INDEX

A

almanacs, 30

atlases, 27–28

B

bibliographies, 27, 40

   entry arrangement examples, 75–80

   research report sample (Australia), 115

   titles in, 76

biographical dictionaries, 36

books, bibliography entry, 75–77

brochures or pamphlets, bibliography entry, 80

C

card catalog, 32

CD-ROMs, 30

   computer software (CD-ROMs, Disks, etc.), bibliography entry, 79

checklist (final copy), 89

citing sources, 48, 71, 72–80, 87

   pictures, 64–65

computer research, 30, 44–50

   "contact us" links, 60

   search engines, 45–48, 96

computer software (CD-ROMs, disks, etc.), bibliography entry, 79

computer stations, 30

cover, 89

D

Dewey Decimal System, 26

dictionaries

   online, 49, 97

   print, 26–27, 29

direct quotations, 42, 68, 71

disks. *SEE* computer software (CD-ROMs, Disks, etc.) bibliography entry

doorknob sign, 94

DVDs, 30

   films (in theaters, on TV, DVDs, or videotape), bibliography entry, 79

E

electronic database, 25

encyclopedias

   online, 49, 50, 97

   print, 27

encyclopedias, bibliography entry, 77

endnotes, 73, 74

   research report sample (Australia), 111–112

F

fact *versus* opinion, 66–69

   game, 101–104

   game score sheet, 104

films (in theaters, on TV, DVDs, or videotape), bibliography entry, 79

filtering (blocking) programs, 30

final copy, 86–90

   checklist, 89

citing sources, 87

cover, 89

graphics in, 88

proofreading, 88

requirements (teacher), 87

title (choosing), 88–89

first (rough) draft, 81–85

    organization (order) examples, 82–84

    writing (getting started), 84–85

footnotes, 73–74

    research report sample (Australia), 113–114

    superscript, 74

G

glossary (research terms), 116–119

graphics, 62–65

    examples, 62

final copy and, 88

SEE ALSO pictures

H

headings (note cards), 41, 42

I

ideas, 16

    main (note cards), 42

SEE ALSO topic selection

index cards. *SEE* notes and note cards

indirect quotations, 68

Internet research, 30, 44–50

    "contact us" links, 60

search engines, 45–48, 96

interviews and interviewing, 51–57

interview sheet sample, 98

    planning, 52–56

    questionnaire form sample, 100

    survey form sample, 99

    surveys and questionnaires, 56–57

interviews (personal), bibliography entry, 78

K

keywords, 27

L

libraries/librarians, 21–23, 24–31

    Dewey Decimal System, 26

library card, 25, 31

M

magazine articles, bibliography entry, 77

magazines. *SEE* newspapers and magazines (periodicals)

media centers/media specialists. *SEE* libraries/librarians

N

newspaper articles, bibliography entry, 77

newspapers and magazines (periodicals), 30

notes and note cards, 39–43

    computer generated, 43

    main ideas, 42

research report sample (Australia), 106–108

sample, 42, 95

taking and making of, 40–43, 48

writing from, 84–85

O

online dictionaries, 49, 97

online encyclopedias, 49, 50, 97

online research, 30, 44–50

"contact us" links, 60

search engines, 45–48, 96

opinion *versus* fact, 66–69

game, 101–104

game score sheet, 104

outlines and outlining, 32–38, 81, 82–84

Leonardo Da Vinci example, 35–37

format, 34

making, 33

master plan, 33

numbering and lettering, 30

organization (order) examples, 82–84

research report sample (Australia), 109

topics (main, sub, detailed), 33–35, 37–38

writing from, 84–85

P

page numbers (note cards), 41, 42

paraphrase, 42

periodicals. *SEE* newspapers and magazines (periodicals)

personal interviews, bibliography entry, 78

photocopies, 25, 43, 64

pictures, 61–65

explanation of, 64–65

place visits (for research), 58–60

plagiarism, 48, 69, 70–71

printing graphics, 49, 64

proofreading, 88

Q

questionnaires, bibliography entry, 78

questionnaires. *SEE* surveys and questionnaires

quotation books, 28

quotation marks, 68, 71

search engines and, 47, 48

quotations

direct, 42, 68, 71

indirect, 68

R

research (report) calendar

blank (two-month), 92–93

sample, 13–14

research report sample (Australia), 105–115

resources. *SEE* sources or resources

revising or rewriting. *SEE* final copy

S

scheduling, 11–14

search engines, 45–48, 96

  free, 45, 96

  quotation marks and, 47, 48

searches (how-to), 46–48

source notes, 73, 74–75

  research report sample (Australia), 110

source number, 40, 41, 42

sources or resources, 21–23, 24–31

  computer research, 44–50

  list of, 40, 41

  place visits (for research), 58–60

  research report list sample (Australia), 105

subject selection. SEE topic selection

surveys and questionnaires, 56–57

  questionnaire form sample, 100

  survey form sample, 99

surveys, bibliography entry, 78

T

television shows, bibliography entry, 79

time budget chart, 12, 91

titles

  in bibliographies, 76

  choosing, 88–89

topic selection, 15–20

  focus sharpening examples, 17–20

  ideas (narrowing), 16

TV. SEE films (in Theaters, on TV, DVDs, or Videotape), bibliography entry

V

videos, 30

videotape. SEE films (in theaters, on TV, DVDs, or videotape), bibliography entry

W

Web sites, 30, 45–50

  "contact us" links, 60

  evaluation of, 48

  pages (download, save, print), 49

  search engines, 45–48, 96

Web sites, bibliography entry, 78–79

writing. SEE final copy; first (rough draft)

Marvin Terban

PHOTO: © KAREN TERBAN

Called a "master of wordplay" and "Mr. English for Kids," Marvin Terban is Dr. Grammar on Scholastic.com. He was born in Chelsea, Massachusetts, and he got his start as an author with *The Fuzzy Green Dragon*, a book he wrote and drew in the first grade. His first real writing job was a weekly column for his local newspaper when he was in high school. He was also the editor of his high school newspaper and literary magazine. He went to Tufts and Columbia universities, where he received Bachelor's and Master's degrees respectively. For over forty years, he has taught English, Latin, public speaking, and theater at the Columbia Grammar and Preparatory School in New York City.

Terban took a break from teaching to produce audio-visual educational programs for children. Returning to the classroom with renewed energy, he developed teaching games that use humor to help students understand and enjoy the mystifying idiosyncrasies of the English language. Those games grew into the highly original series of funny books on English for which he is known.

Terban's books have made it as far as Shanghai University in China, where they are used to teach English to adults. His Scholastic *Dictionary of Idioms* has been translated into Japanese and Korean. Two of his books were turned into early computer games. He and his wife, Karen, a former special education instructor, also wrote two activity books for teachers. His Scholastic books *Checking Your Grammar* and *Dictionary of Idioms* have sold well over one million copies each.

Terban has acted in local community theater plays to raise money for charitable causes. He has also had small parts in movies directed by Woody Allen. For many summers he directed plays at a children's sleep-away camp. He has paid "Meet the Author" visits to schools, colleges, and conferences all over the United States, South America, Europe, Israel, and Japan. Marvin and Karen Terban live in New York City in a rambling apartment across from Central Park. They have two children, David and Jennifer, both computer digital artists, and a frisky cat named Tiger.

NOTES

NOTES